W9-CEW-724

Sentences

Circle the sentences.

1. in the sandbox

2. across the street

3. she went into the store

4. my best friend

5. this is a pretty hat

6. do you want some ice cream

7. at 6:00

8. the clown did a funny trick

9. he flew his airplane

10. this red bird

11. let's paint the house green

12. his dog played ball

13. in my pocket

14. put your coat on that chair

How many sentences did you find? _____

Name _____

 Find the Sentences

Circle each sentence.

1. the bear ate the five big fish

2. one sunny day

3. to play ball

4. down the street

5. a yellow kitten went up the tree

6. a little boy ran

7. under the red and white blanket

8. six birds flew

9. to catch the dog

10. see that funny

11. will you come to my house

12. mother called the boys

13. let's go now

14. in the park

How many sentences did you find? _____

     Punctuation EMC 141

Is It a Sentence?

Write **yes** or **no** on the line.

1. Sam and Kim played ball.   ___yes___

2. Went up the hill.   _____

3. The class went to the library.   _____

4. Tanya ate her lunch.   _____

5. Susan, Ann, and Jim.   _____

6. The flag waved in the wind.   _____

7. A funny clown.   _____

8. My sister gave me her bike.   _____

9. The gift was from Pete.   _____

10. Did a good job.   _____

11. Carl's pet dog.   _____

12. That mouse ran under my bed.   _____

13. The band marched in the parade.   _____

14. Down the street.   _____

How many sentences did you find? _____

Name _____

Begin with a Capital Letter

Begin each sentence with a capital letter.

T

1. ~~t~~ed likes to play baseball.

2. the oldest boy.

3. my pet hamster got out of its cage.

4. we all helped wash the car.

5. under the bed.

6. the giraffe ate from the top of the tree.

7. can you fix the broken toy?

8. margo and her pet dog

9. we ran down the street.

10. will you order a big pizza?

Punctuation EMC 141

Begin with a Capital Letter

Put a capital letter at the beginning of each sentence.
Put an X on groups of words that are not sentences.

the beaver wanted to build a lodge.

she cut down trees and branches.

a big pile in the pond.

the lodge stuck up above the water.

doorway under the water.

the beaver went into the dry lodge.

this is where the beaver will have her babies.

Telling Sentences

Put a ● at the end of each sentence that tells something.

1. A little kite blew across the sky

2. Big and little kites

3. Fell from the sky

4. My kite was broken

5. I must get a new kite

6. A big, red kite

Write a sentence that tells something about a kite.

_____

_____

_____

_____

_____

_____

Name _____

Statement

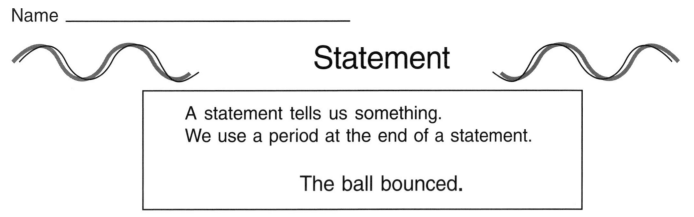

> A statement tells us something.
> We use a period at the end of a statement.
>
> The ball bounced.

Put a period at the end of each statement.

1. I am Jim

2. My brother is Mark

3. We live on Elm Street

4. In a green house

5. Will be ten on Saturday

6. We are going to the park

7. We will have a picnic and play games

8. The cake will look like

9. Mark likes space movies

10. He wants to be an astronaut

Write a sentence that tells something about an astronaut.

_____

_____

       Punctuation EMC 141

Name _____

Asking Sentences

A question mark is used at the end
of a sentence that asks something.

Where are you going?

Put a **?** at the end of the "asking" sentences.

1. Can Bob ride a bike**?**

2. Do you want to go to my house

3. Can we go to the park

4. Was the cat furry

5. That is my toy bear

6. What is that

7. Where do you live

8. We made popcorn

9. Is it going to rain tomorrow

10. What is your name

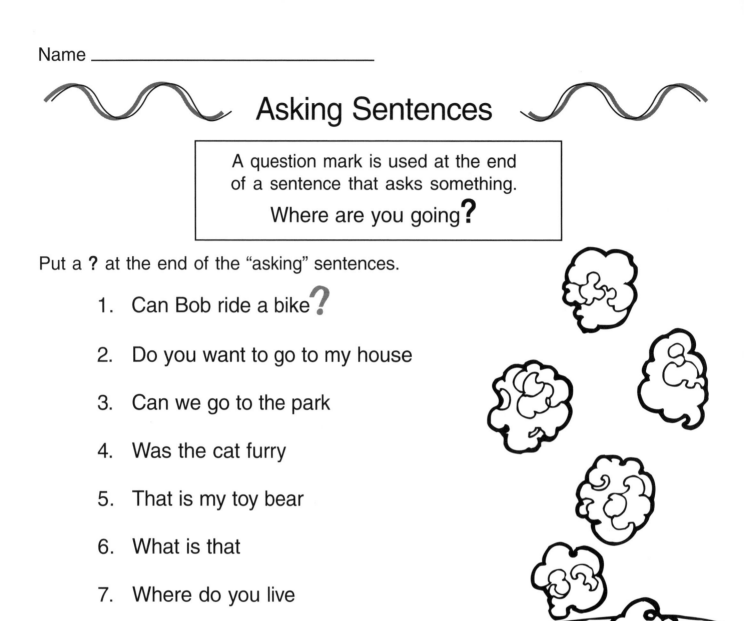

Write an asking question about popcorn.

_____

_____

_____

_____

                                       Punctuation EMC 141

Name _____

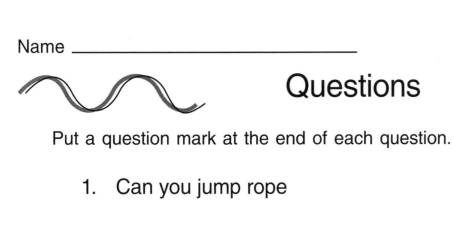

Questions

Put a question mark at the end of each question.

1. Can you jump rope

2. Do you like to go to the zoo

3. I saw a lizard in my yard

4. Can we have pizza for dinner

5. We will go to the pet shop

6. I like that little brown puppy

7. When can you come over to my house

8. Is that your mother

Write a question about a funny monkey.

_____

_____

_____

_____

9   Punctuation EMC 141

Name _____

Questions and Answers

Put question marks at the end of sentences that ask something. Answer the questions with a statement.

1. How many pets do you have

_____

2. My home is painted blue

_____

3. How old are you

_____

4. What is your favorite color

_____

5. He likes ice cream

_____

6. Where do you live

_____

                   Punctuation EMC 141

Name _____

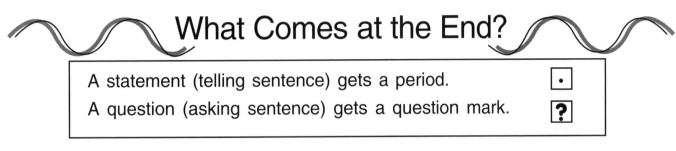

What Comes at the End?

| A statement (telling sentence) gets a period. | . |
| A question (asking sentence) gets a question mark. | ? |

Match:

1. I like to play hopscotch   •

2. Can you run fast   •

3. Morris has a pet frog   •

4. What is in that box   •

5. Alma has a baby sister   **?**

6. Where did the puppy go   **?**

7. Will you help me   **?**

8. Sandy went swimming   **?**

                                                   Punctuation EMC 141

Name _____

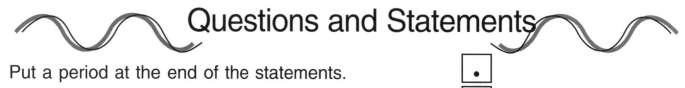 # Questions and Statements

Put a period at the end of the statements.

Put a question mark at the end of the questions.

1. Who is going to the zoo with us

2. We will meet Bobby and Tamara at the zoo

3. Do you like snakes

4. Gorillas scare me

5. Tamara saw a baby hippo in the water

6. Can monkeys climb that tall tree

7. How many tigers are in the cage

8. Have you seen the dolphin show

9. Which animal did you like best

10. Elephants are gigantic animals

11. That chimp makes me laugh

12. What time is it

13. We have to be home by 6:00

14. Can we come again next Saturday

Draw your favorite zoo animal on the back of this paper.

   Punctuation EMC 141

Write About Me

Start at a.
Connect the dots to find the hidden animal.

Write a statement about this animal.

Write a question about this animal.

Lunch Time

Put a period at the end of the statements.

Put a question mark at the end of the questions.

I had a good nap

Now I am hungry

I want something to eat

Is there food under the table

I think I saw some crumbs there

The cat is by the door

Is he asleep

He looks like he is

Can I sneak by the cat

Will he wake up when I go by

He may be hungry too

Write about what you think will happen next.

_____

_____

_____

Name _____

 # An Ant Picnic

1. Read the story.
2. Punctuate the sentences.

Do you like summer

It is my favorite time of year

Can you guess why

I love picnics

So do all my friends

Have you ever gone on a picnic

What food did you take

Did you drop scraps on the ground

We find good food when people leave

Look for me at your next picnic

Do you think I will be there

Draw a picnic lunch on the tablecloth.

Name _____

Exclamation Mark

> This is an exclamation mark. **!**
> An exclamation shows strong feeling.

Put an **!** at the end of each of these exclamations.

1. Stop that cat **!**

2. This house is a mess

3. We need help

4. I hate pickles

5. Be careful

6. Stop fighting

Write a sentence that needs an exclamation mark.

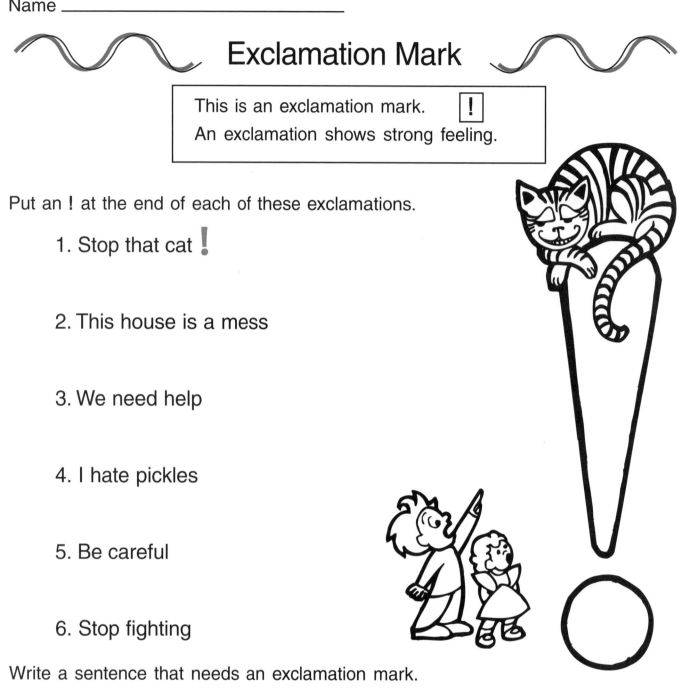

_____

_____

_____

_____

16 Punctuation EMC 141

Name _____

Find the Exclamations

Put an **!** at the end of sentences that show strong feelings.
Put an **X** on the sentences that don't need an exclamation mark.

1. Stop that

2. Is that flower beautiful

3. I must go

4. Don't touch it

5. Wow

6. Ouch, that hurt

7. Do you want it

8. I'll rest now

9. Stop that thief

10. Can you come here

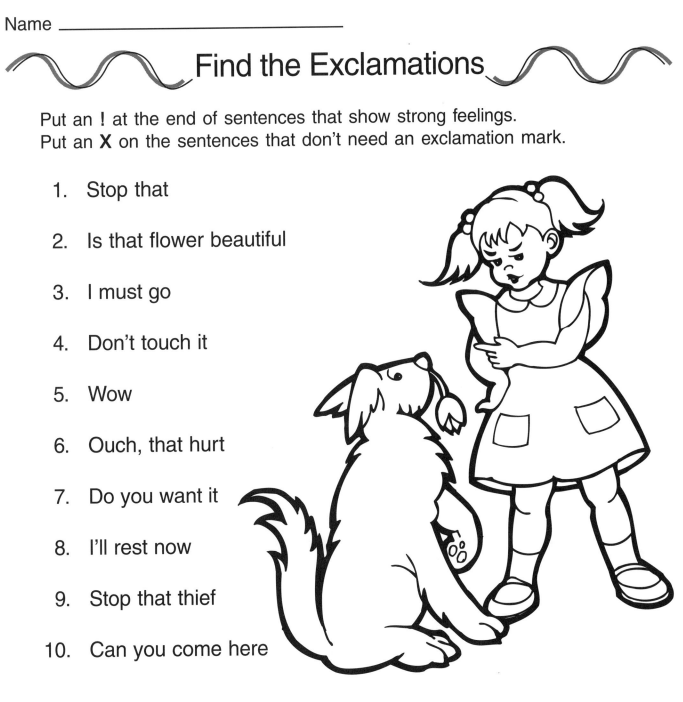

Write a sentence that needs an exclamation mark.

_____

_____

_____

17   Punctuation EMC 141

Name _____

Punctuation

Every sentence needs a punctuation mark.

period	Pizza tastes good.
question mark	Do you like pizza?
exclamation mark	This pizza is too hot!

1. Did you bring your lunch today

2. All of the library books were due today

3. Put that down right now

4. Haven't you finished your homework yet

5. Come over here

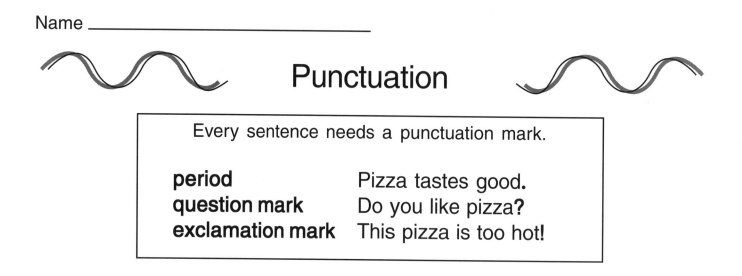

6. Did you have fun at the party

7. That movie was really scary

8. Where do you live

Punctuation EMC 141

Name _____

Picnic at the Park

1. Read the groups of words.
2. If the group of words is not a sentence, cross it out.
3. If the group of words is a sentence, put in the right punctuation.

Carlos and Mario went on a picnic

They put their food on the picnic table

Just as they started to eat a storm started

The food began to get wet

Raindrops, raindrops, raindrops

The boys ran for shelter

Hurrah, the rain stopped

Could the boys eat lunch now

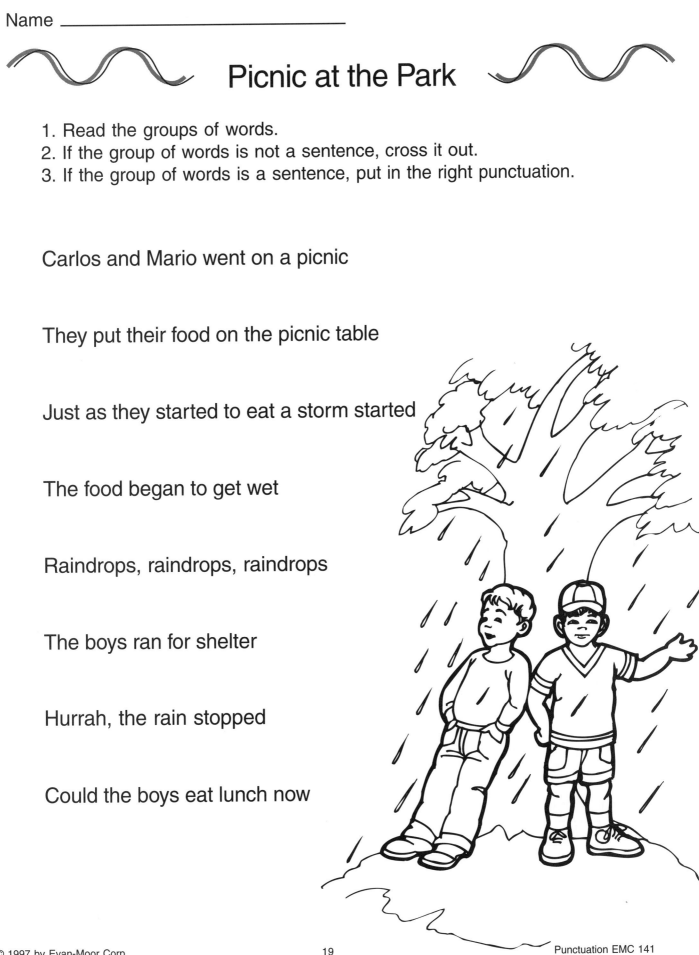

Punctuation EMC 141

Name _____

Write Your Own Sentences

Write sentences about this picture.
Use the correct end punctuation and capital letters.

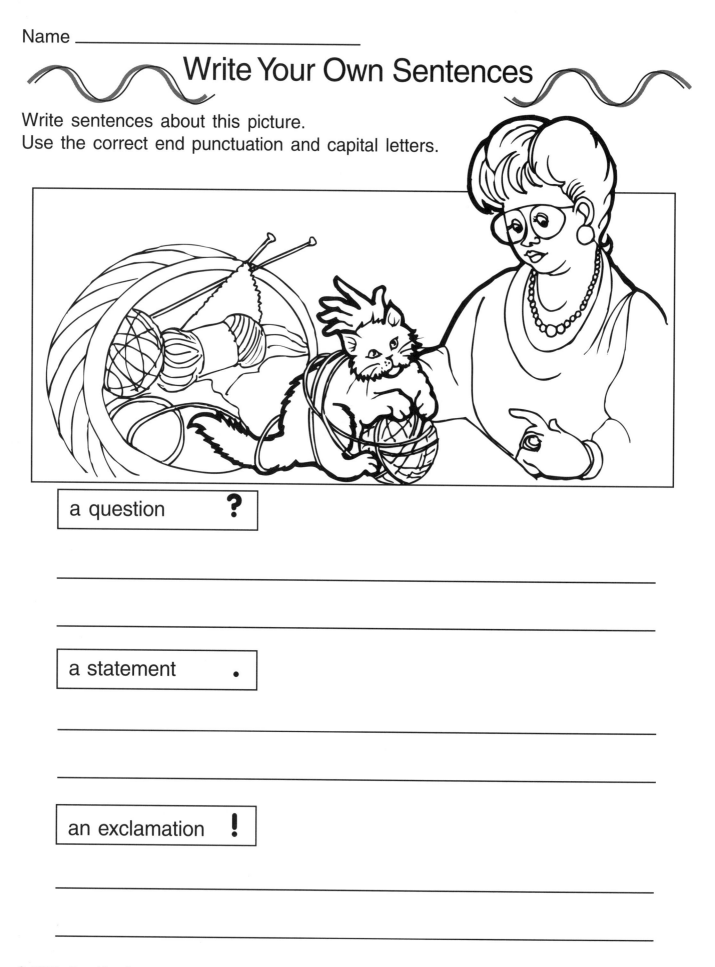

| a question | **?** |

_____

_____

| a statement | **.** |

_____

_____

| an exclamation | **!** |

_____

_____

 Punctuation EMC 141

Name _____

At the Beach

1. Read the story.
2. Punctuate the sentences.

What is your favorite
day of the week

I like Saturday best
My friend Tony and I go to the
beach
We climb on the rocks and make
sand castles

Are you a good climber

I am a good climber

We like to look in the tide pools

We find interesting plants and animals

Have you ever seen
a live crab

Tony found one last week
Did you know crabs could pinch
Tony dropped that crab very fast
I got too close to the waves last Saturday

Tony yelled, "Look out "
It was too late
Boy, did I get wet

Do you want to go with us next time
Will your mom let you come
We will let you pick up any crabs we find
We will have a good time

Punctuation EMC 141

Name _____

Snow Fun

1. Read the story.
2. Punctuate the sentences.

Look

It's snowing

Winter is here at last

It is cold outside in the snow

Do you have mittens to keep your fingers warm

I have red wool mittens

What kind do you have

Do you have boots and a hat too

Can you come to my house to play

Bring your sled

We can slide down the hill by the school

We can make a snow monster later

Will your mom let you come

Come on, Mike

Let's go ask her now

Draw a snow monster on the back of this paper.

22

Name _____

 # Popcorn!

1. Read the story.
2. Punctuate the sentences.

I want some popcorn

Mom isn't here

Can we fix it

Sure, I know how

I'll get the popper

You get the popcorn

Is the popper turned on

I plugged it in

Will you put in a cup of

popcorn now

I'll melt some butter

Wow

Look at it pop

It smells so good

Do you want to eat it outside

That will be fun

I'll put the butter on it

Don't forget the salt

I can't wait to taste it

Draw your favorite snack on the back of this paper.

23 Punctuation EMC 141

Name _____

 A Trip to the Pet Shop

1. Read the story.
2. Punctuate the sentences.

Mom, are you going to town today

I want to go to the pet shop

My fish need food

May I ask Kim to go with us

She likes to see the animals there

Do you see all the new kittens

Aren't they cute

Which one do you like best

I like the little one with the black nose

Oops He fell on top of the yellow one

This is all the fish food I need

Should I get a new bowl too

I think I'll wait until next time

Come on, Kim

We had better hurry

My mom will be waiting for us

This has been fun

Are you going to come back for a kitten

Punctuation EMC 141

Name _____

Lost Frogs

1. Read the story.
2. Punctuate the sentences.

Why are you laughing

What is so funny

Miss Brown brought three frogs to school

She put them in a glass box

We named them Ribbit, Hopper, and Max

That doesn't sound

very funny

What happened

Pam went to see the frogs

The lid was off the box

Max and Hopper got away

They hopped out the door and down the hall

That is funny

Who left the lid off

We don't know

Can you go to the pond with me

Maybe we can get more frogs

Ribbit needs friends

Draw Miss Brown chasing the frogs out the door.

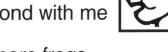

Name _____

Pumpkin's Adventure

1. Read the story.
2. Punctuate the sentences.

What a surprise I had yesterday

It was a cool day in October

I was growing in my pumpkin patch

Two children came over and picked me up

What was going to happen next

Why did they want me

The boy carried me to his wagon

The children began to pull me down the street

Where were they taking me

We came to a house with a wide porch

The boy cut holes in my side

Then the girl put a candle inside me

They sat me in this window

Why did they leave me here

It is very dark outside

Oh, no

Who are those monsters tapping at the door

Draw a picture of the monsters on the back of this paper.

 Punctuation EMC 141

Name _____

Commands

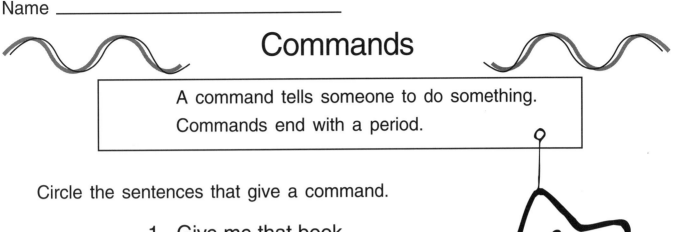

A command tells someone to do something.
Commands end with a period.

Circle the sentences that give a command.

1. Give me that book.

2. That cake looks delicious.

3. Bring me my new shoes.

4. My bicycle is red and black.

5. How do you get to the mall from here?

6. Put your toys away.

7. This is too hot.

8. Get out of the street.

9. Stay away from that broken glass.

10. Don't put your feet on the coffee table.

11. What are you going to do this afternoon?

12. Do your homework before you go out to play.

27

Name _____

What Kind of Sentence Is It?

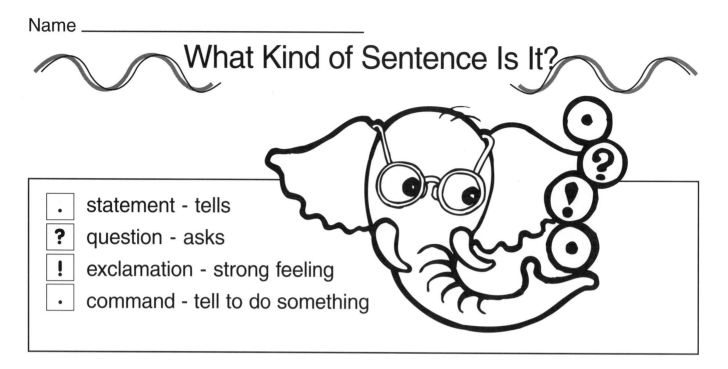

.	statement - tells
?	question - asks
!	exclamation - strong feeling
.	command - tell to do something

Punctuate each sentence.
Tell what type of sentence it is.

1. What time do we catch the train   _____

2. Let's meet at the park   _____

3. Don't leave your toys on the floor   _____

4. This is hard work   _____

5. Wow, what a surprise   _____

6. Mario and Marta went to Disneyland _____

7. Can you help me fix this   _____

8. Put that away before you leave   _____

28

Four Kinds of Sentences

statement — I like you.

question — Do you like me?

exclamation — Don't run away!

command — Sit down!

Put the correct punctuation at the end of the sentences.
Tell which type of sentence it is.

1. I hate creamed spinach **!**   exclamation

2. Can you explain how to do this problem _____

3. Put those books on the shelf _____

4. Don't put your feet on the furniture _____

5. Let's go to Jamal's house _____

6. Ouch, that really hurt _____

7. What time do you have to go home _____

8. They went to Mexico for Easter _____

29

Name _____

The Job

Write sentences about this picture.

| a question | ? |

_____

_____

| a statement or command | . |

_____

_____

| an exclamation | ! |

_____

_____

       Punctuation EMC 141

Name _____

Using Capital Letters

A sentence starts with a capital letter.

Fill in the capital letters with a green crayon.

M

1. my pet is small.

2. it can hop and swim.

3. my pet eats bugs.

4. it is as green as grass.

5. it is a funny pet.

6. can you tell what my pet is?

Start at A. Connect the capital letters.

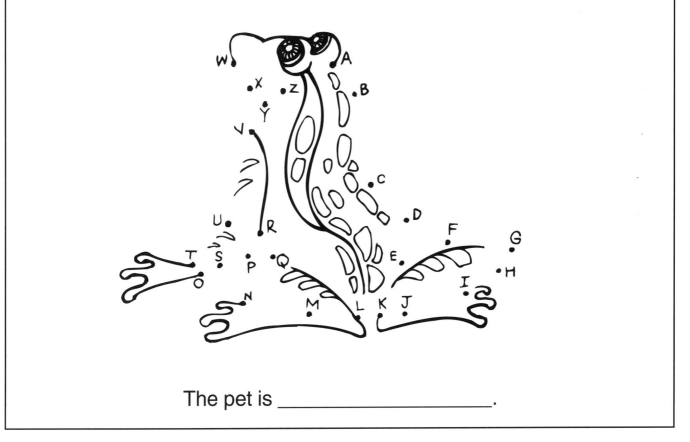

The pet is _____.

31   Punctuation EMC 141

Name _____

Punctuate the Sentences

Read the sentences out loud.
Put a punctuation mark at the end of each sentence.
Put a capital at the beginning of each sentence.

M   **W**

1. my dog is a poodle. what kind do you have?

2. is that a cat no, it is a skunk

3. bob can't find his cake did Ann eat it

4. why did you miss school were you sick

5. do you like to play hopscotch i think it's fun

6. when did you get that toy can I play with it

7. they must go home at 4:30 what time is it now

8. grandma is coming today she will stay a week

9. how old are you i am 10

10. i am going to the movies can you come

Name _____

Correct These Sentences

Put a capital letter at the beginning of each sentence.
Put a punctuation mark at the end of each sentence.

1. where did you get that book can I read it

2. i just got to school am I late

3. john has a sandwich for lunch what do you have

4. don't climb up that old ladder it isn't safe

5. i like the present you made for me

6. when are you going to the party can I come too

7. my dentist gave me a new toothbrush

8. raul fell off his bike he broke his arm

9. who painted that picture it is pretty

10. please bring me that vase i want to put these flowers in it

33 Punctuation EMC 141

Name _____

 # Maggie's Lost Mice

Punctuate the sentences in this story.
Put a capital letter at the beginning of each sentence.

1. C
   ~~c~~an you come over ? I i need help .

2. my pet mice escaped can you help me catch them

3. where do you think they went did they get outside

4. look out one just ran under your feet

5. did it go under that chair let's move it and see

6. i got him where is the cage

7. how many mice do you have we've found three

8. that is all lock the cage carefully

9. would you like to feed them they like sunflower seeds

10. thank you for helping you're a good friend

                   Punctuation EMC 141

Name _____

Capital I

| The word I is always capitalized. |

Copy the sentences.
Use capital letters where they are needed.

1. can i go out to play?

_____

2. amy and i gave the dog a bath.

_____

3. i like to eat ice cream.

_____

4. mom says i have to stay home today.

_____

5. when will i get to have a turn?

_____

6. my sister and i are twins.

_____

| Write a sentence with the word I. |
| _____ |

     Punctuation EMC 141

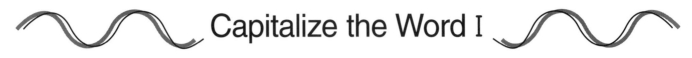

Capitalize the Word I

Capitalize the word **I** every time you see it in this story.

When i was little i played a color game with my mother.

Every time i saw the color red i would shout "i spy red!"

Every day we would look for another color. This is how i

learned the names of all the colors.

i still like to look for colors when i take a walk. Only now

i look for colors of cars and trucks. It is only a few more

years before i can drive a car. i'm already looking for the

best color. Maybe i'll get a red one, since it was the first

color i ever knew!

Name _____

Trapped!

1. Read.
2. Punctuate.
3. Capitalize.

help i can't get away i am trapped in this net

will help come soon how will i escape it's no fun to be

in a net

i want to be back in the water

what is that it is a rip in the net can i get out that way

the rip isn't big will i be able to push my way out

i'm going to try here i go

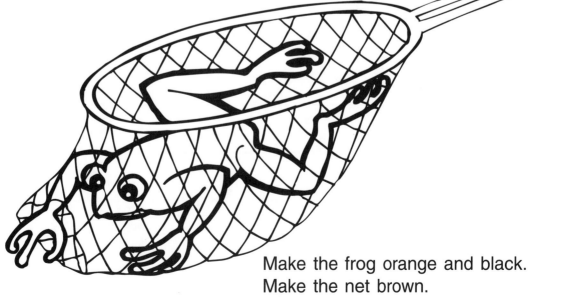

Make the frog orange and black.
Make the net brown.
Make the water blue and green.

         Punctuation EMC 141

Name _____

Nightmares!

1. Read.
2. Punctuate.
3. Capitalize.

what a strange place this is it doesn't look like Earth

why is it so dark what is that furry shape over there by the

rocks it's moving closer help i can't get away why won't my

feet move i'm caught in sticky mud can anyone hear me hurry

save me what a scary dream i am glad i

woke up i'm never going to eat a peanut

butter and pickle sandwich again

Write about a scary dream you have had.
Use capital letters and punctuation marks.

_____

_____

_____

_____

Name _____

Names Start with
Capital Letters

ABCDEFGHIJKLMNOPQRSTUVWXYZ

Write the names with capital letters in the right places.

sally smith   _____

jamal biondi   _____

raul martinez   _____

anna chin   _____

salvatore toscano   _____

tammy westwood   _____

esther jacobs   _____

mary beth allen   _____

My name is   _____

                                       Punctuation EMC 141

Name _____

Capitalize Names

Copy the sentences. Capitalize the names.

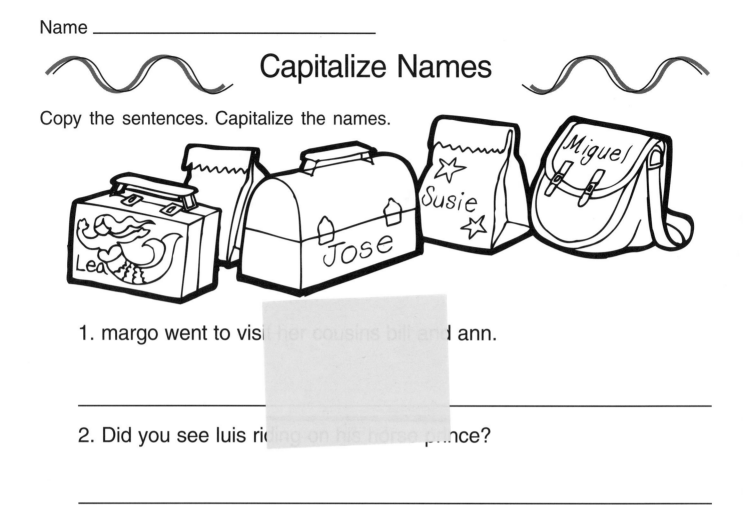

1. margo went to visit her cousins bill and ann.

_____

2. Did you see luis riding on his horse prince?

_____

3. columbus sailed across the atlantic ocean.

_____

4. doctor reyes gave kathy a shot.

_____

5. Can you help mrs. smith mow her lawn?

_____

6. roy, tim, and bill are triplets.

_____

   Punctuation EMC 141

Name _____

Sam's Pets

Read the story.
Capitalize the names.

sam has two dogs.

One is a black and white dog named lady.

The other dog is a frisky puppy named bubbles.

bubbles likes to play with lady.

Sometimes lady gets tired of bubbles.

She growls and moves away.

bubbles will follow lady and try to play again.

sam has to take bubbles to the front yard

so lady can get some rest.

 Punctuation EMC 141

Name _____

Happy Birthday to You

1. Read.
2. Punctuate.
3. Capitalize.

| Mom |

tommy, your birthday is almost here you

may invite five friends to your party what

do you want to do would you like a party

at home i can bake a cake, and you can

play games choose soon so we can send

out the invitations

| Tommy |

could we go somewhere henry took us to

the pizza place on his birthday it was fun

i've got an idea i would like to take my

friends roller-skating can we do that could

we come home after we skate for ice

cream and cake i can't wait aren't

birthdays wonderful

You are invited!

Punctuation EMC 141

Name _____

A Turn at Bat

1. Read.
2. Punctuate.
3. Capitalize.

it is matt's turn at bat will he get a hit

matt hit the ball hard look at it go

it is going to the back of the field run fast,

matt ted is running after the ball can he

catch it will matt make a home run oh, no

ted got the ball matt is not happy to be out

it is my turn at bat will i get a hit

i want to make a run for my team i will do my best

Write what you think will happen next.
Use capital letters and punctuation marks.

_____

_____

_____

Name _____

Days of the Week

Days of the week start with capital letters.

Write the days of the week in the blanks.

1. We go to church_____morning.
   sunday

2. Mr. Lee missed work_____and_____.
   thursday   friday

3. Can you come to the park with me on_____?
   saturday

4. I had to do a lot of homework_____night.
   monday

5. Ahmed's dentist appointment is_____at 3:00.
   wednesday

6. Let's go fishing_____after school.
   tuesday

Today is_____.

Name _____

Months of the Year

| The names of the month begin with capital letters. |

Write each month.
Begin with a capital letter.

january _____   july _____

february _____   august _____

march _____   september _____

april _____   october _____

may _____   november _____

june _____   december _____

What month is it? _____

         Punctuation EMC 141

Name _____

Capitalize the names of holidays.

Put capital letters where they are needed.

1. we will spend christmas in texas with grandmother.

2. terry gave me a funny card on valentine's day.

3. we had a fat turkey for thanksgiving dinner.

4. are you going to have fireworks on independence day?

5. mark gave his dad a tie for father's day.

6. mr. barton's class is learning about chinese new year.

7. do you look for colored eggs on easter sunday?

8. we remember george washington and abraham lincoln on

   presidents' day.

Place Names

| Place names begin with capital letters. |

Write the capital letters for these place names.

marine world   _____

yosemite national park   _____

san francisco   _____

mississippi river   _____

bagel bakery   _____

museum of natural history   _____

jefferson elementary school   _____

new york   _____

british columbia   _____

quick stop gas   _____

broadway avenue   _____

Name _____

Place Names

Capitalize the names of places.

1. In fairbanks, alaska, snow stays on the mountains most of the year.

2. I went swimming in lake tahoe with my best friend.

3. The library is on elm street.

4. Tomorrow we will go to chicago to see a ball game.

5. Larry was fishing off the wharf in monterey.

6. Stella traveled to seattle, washington, with her family.

Write a sentence about a place you have visited.
Remember to use capital letters.

_____

_____

_____

_____

_____

Name _____

Using Capital Letters

A B C D E F G

> • people and place names
> • the word I
> • days, months, holidays
> • cities, states, countries

Write the sentences and put in the missing capital letters.

1. pedro lives in santa monica, california.

_____

_____

2. carla said, "i am going to six flags over texas in august."

_____

_____

3. mrs. williams was born in utah, but now she lives in mexico city.

_____

_____

4. can i ask tony and his family over for easter dinner?

_____

_____

49   Punctuation EMC 141

Name _____

Commas

Put commas where they belong.

1. Columbus Ohio

2. Honolulu Hawaii

3. Toronto Ontario

4. Memphis Tennessee

5. Santa Barbara California

6. Whitehorse Yukon Territory

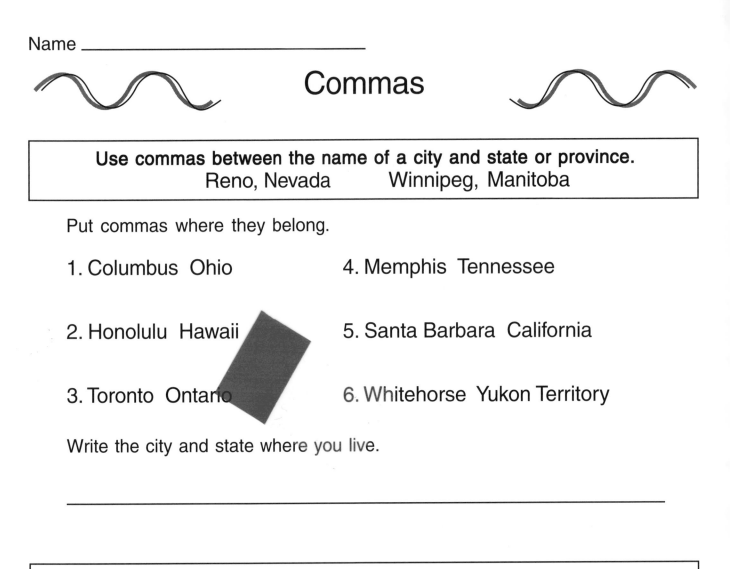

Write the city and state where you live.

_____

Use commas between the day and the year
May 5, 1996

Put commas in these dates.

1. March 31 1874

2. July 4 1776

3. January 1 1998

4. December 25 2000

5. August 22 1943

6. November 3 1800

Write the month, day, and year you were born.

_____

Name _____

 # Writing Dates

Here is Annie's calendar for March 1998.

Sun.	Mon.	Tues.	Wed.	Thur.	Fri.	Sat.
	1	2	3	4 music lesson	5	6 sleep over at Tanisha's
7	8	9	10	11 doctor appointment	12	13
14	15 Father's birthday	16	17	18 music lesson	19	20
21	22	23	24	25	26	27
28 sing at church	29	30	31			

Answer each question.
Give the complete date.

1. When is Annie's doctor appointment? _____

2. When is Annie going to sleep over at Tanisha's house? _____

3. When is her father's birthday? _____

4. What day is she singing at church? _____

5. On what two dates does she have music lessons? _____

Name _____

Commas in a List

Use commas to separate three or more items in a list.

apple, orange, and peach   shirt, hat, and pants

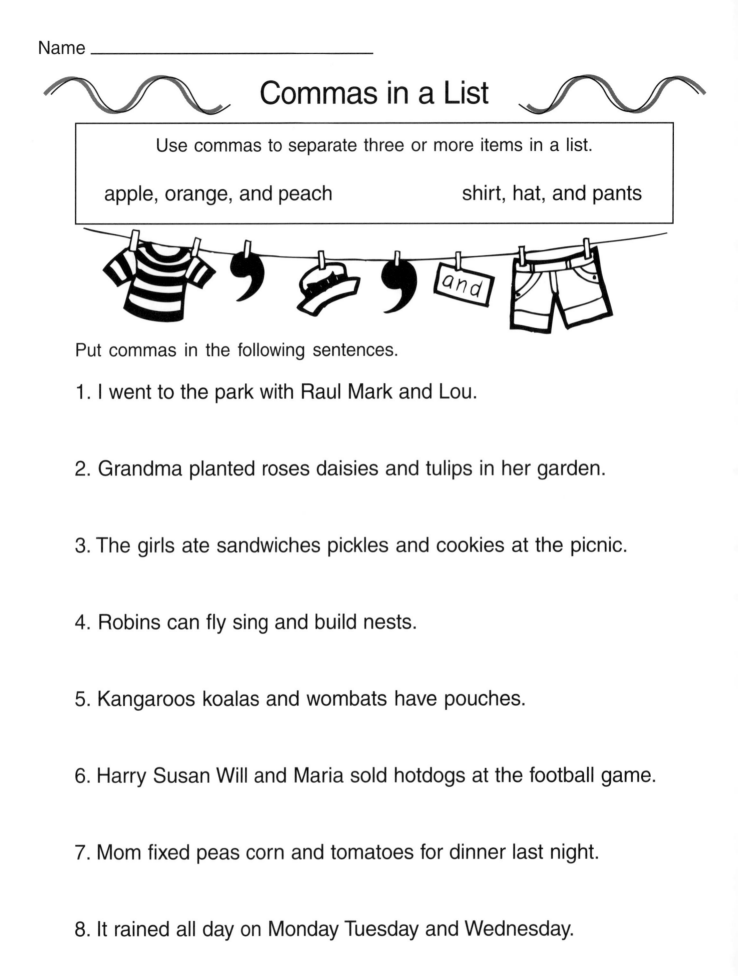

Put commas in the following sentences.

1. I went to the park with Raul Mark and Lou.

2. Grandma planted roses daisies and tulips in her garden.

3. The girls ate sandwiches pickles and cookies at the picnic.

4. Robins can fly sing and build nests.

5. Kangaroos koalas and wombats have pouches.

6. Harry Susan Will and Maria sold hotdogs at the football game.

7. Mom fixed peas corn and tomatoes for dinner last night.

8. It rained all day on Monday Tuesday and Wednesday.

                                       Punctuation EMC 141

Write Words in a Series

Write a sentence to explain each list.
Use commas to separate the items.

1. Tell what Clarence will do at camp.

swim
ride
hike

_____
_____
_____

2. Tell what Mrs. Chin has in her purse.

a wallet
a comb
a mirror
a lipstick

_____
_____
_____

3. Tell what Mark has in his lunch.

a sandwich
carrot sticks
an apple
cookies

_____
_____
_____

4. Tell what Lonnie got for her birthday.

a story book
a bracelet
cowboy boots
a hamster

_____
_____
_____

Name _____

Add the Commas

Use commas between three or more items in a series.

1. Mosquitos crickets and owls kept the campers awake most of the night.

2. We ate turkey dressing and gravy at Thanksgiving dinner.

3. I want to plant lettuce carrots radishes and peas in my garden.

4. Lightning flashed thunder roared and gusty winds blew during the storm.

5. The children ran through the gate across the lawn and into the house.

6. Would you prefer an apple an orange or a banana in your lunch?

7. Did you go to Disneyland Magic Mountain or Marine World on your vacation?

8. Whales sharks tuna and jellyfish all live in the sea.

Name _____

Using Commas
in Sentences

Put commas in the right places as you write your own sentences.

1. Write a sentence about your favorite foods.
    Use at least three things in a series.

    _____

    _____

    _____

2. Write a sentence about your friends.
    Use at least three names in a series.

    _____

    _____

    _____

3. Write a sentence about animals.
    Put at least three things in a series.

    _____

    _____

    _____

4. Write a sentence about what you like to do.
    Put at least three things in a series.

    _____

    _____

    _____

Write a Story

Look at this picture.

Write a story about it.

Use correct punctuation and capital letters.

_____

_____

_____

_____

_____

_____

_____

Punctuation EMC 141

Name _____

Writing an Address

Use capital letters and commas to address the envelopes.

Write this address
on the envelope.

washington elementary school
1200 main street
madera california 93637

Write this address
on the envelope.

mr frank jones
537 yosemite avenue
eaton colorado 80615

Write your
school
address on
this envelope.

Punctuation EMC 141

Name _____

Commas in a Friendly Letter

Put a comma after the greeting.
Put a comma after the closing.

Copy these greetings.
Use capital letters.
Write the commas after the greeting.

1. dear grandma and grandpa

_____

2. dear juanita

_____

3. dear aunt mattie

_____

4. dear conrad

_____

5. dear uncle fred

_____

6. dear george

_____

Copy these closings.
Use capital letters.
Write the commas after the closing.

1. love

_____

2. sincerely

_____

3. your friend

_____

4. goodbye

_____

58

Name _____

Writing Greetings and Closings

Write the greeting and a closing for these letters.
Don't forget the commas.

Hello

Good-bye

1. to your favorite aunt or uncle:

   greeting _____

   closing _____

2. to your teacher:

   greeting _____

   closing _____

3. to your best friend:

   greeting _____

   closing _____

4. to your grandpa:

   greeting _____

   closing _____

 # Correct the Letter

Punctuate the following letter.
Put in the capital letters.

february 18 1997

dear sally

thank you for asking me to your valentine's day party last saturday it was fun playing games with ann margaret tonya and you it was fun making valentine cards too did you have a good time

i really liked the pink ice cream and punch those heart-shaped cookies mrs. ramirez made were so pretty they tasted yummy too do you think ann got to help her mom make them

my mom says i can have a party on saint patrick's day can you come we will play games and have good things to eat

your friend

angela

Punctuation EMC 141

Name _____

A Friendly Letter

Write a friendly letter to someone in your family or to a friend.
Use commas correctly in the greeting and closing.

_____
date

_____
greeting

_____

_____

_____

_____

_____

_____

_____
closing

_____
your name

                                       Punctuation EMC 141

Name _____

Colons

| A colon is used between the hour and the minutes in time. |
| 5:00 |

Copy these times.
Put in the colons.

1. 6 4 5 _____   4. 9 0 0 _____

2. 1 1 2 5 _____   5. 2 3 0 _____

3. 3 1 5 _____   6. 8 5 3 _____

Punctuate the sentences.
Use capital letters where they are needed.

1. arturo has an appointment with dr. martin at 4 15

2. the movie starts at 6 00 don't be late

3. can you get here by 12 00 noon

4. i went to bed at 9 00 last night i got up at 7 30 this morning

5. the plane from new york city will arrive at 2 40

6. sam was born at 12 45 his twin brother was born 15 minutes later

Name _____

Punctuation in Letters

- A comma is used after the greeting in a friendly letter.
- A colon is used after the greeting in a business letter.
- A comma is used after the closing in all letters.

Copy these greetings.
Add the correct punctuation and capital letters.

1. dear mr. president

_____

2. dear cary

_____

3. dear senator kennedy

_____

4. dear santa claus

_____

5. dear governor wilson

_____

6. dear uncle marcus

_____

Write a friendly greeting. _____

Write a business greeting. _____

Write a closing. _____

Name _____

Use the Correct Punctuation

- A comma is used to separate a city and state or province. **Monterey, California**
- A comma is used in dates. **January 1, 1999**
- A colon is used in time. **11:30**
- A period is used in money. **$12.25**

Add the missing punctuation marks.

1. Seattle Washington

2. April 4 1776

3. 1 45

4. Calgary Alberta

5. $1 45

6. February 14 1990

7. 12 30

8. $11 95

9. Denver Colorado

10. $240 60

11. November 17 1996

12. 4 15

Copy this short paragraph.
Fill in the missing punctuation marks.

I am leaving for Albany New York The flight leaves at 6 45 on

May 21 1998 My ticket cost $325 50.

_____

_____

_____

_____

Name _____

Apostrophe

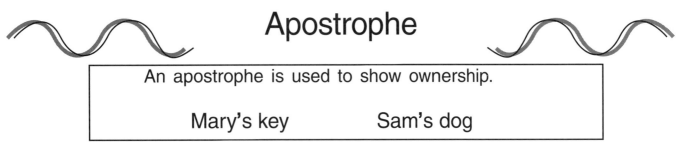

An apostrophe is used to show ownership.

Mary's key   Sam's dog

Label each possession.
Be sure to use an '.

1. Sam _____

2. Pam _____

3. Ken _____

4. Pete _____

5. Lucy _____

6. Arturo _____

Name _____

More Than
One Owner

When plural noun ends in **s**, put the apostrophe after the **s**.

Write a word to show ownership.

1. The tennis balls belonged to the boys.

   the _____ tennis balls

2. The dishes belonged to the cooks.

   the _____ dishes

3. The trucks belonged to the farmers.

   the _____ trucks

4. The cookies belonged to the girls

   the _____ cookies

5. The plants belonged to the gardeners.

   the _____ plants

6. The tools belonged to the workers.

   the _____ tools

 Punctuation EMC 141

Punctuation in Contractions

> An apostrophe is used in contractions.
> can't   I'll   it's

Put in the missing apostrophes.

cant	wont	lets	hes
its	theyre	youll	wouldnt
were	shell	Im	theres

Write the contraction on the correct line.

1. can not _____

2. we are _____

3. I am _____

4. will not _____

5. it is _____

6. there is _____

7. let us _____

8. she will _____

9. would not _____

10. he is _____

11. they are _____

12. you will _____

         Punctuation EMC 141

Name _____

Missing Apostrophes

Copy the sentences.
Write in the missing apostrophes.

1. The two girls sweaters looked the same.

_____

2. That boys dog cant come in the house.

_____

3. We wont go to my aunts house until Friday.

_____

4. Its too late to play with Kates kite.

_____

5. Those workers tools must be put away.

_____

6. I dont like to eat lima beans.

_____

> Circle the contractions in **red**.
> Circle the words that show ownership in **green**.

68   Punctuation EMC 141

Name _____

Punctuation
Abbreviations

An abbreviation is a short way to say something.
Use a period at the end of an abbreviation.

Doctor - Dr.   Avenue - Ave.

Put a period at the end of each abbreviation.
Match it to its long form.

Mr   Doctor

Ave   inch

Dr   Mister

in   Avenue

St   quart

tsp   Governor

qt   Street

Gov   December

Sat   teaspoon

Dec   Saturday

69

Name _____

What Is Missing?

Punctuate the following sentences.
Put in the missing capital letters.

1. mr garcia teaches math at my school

2. max gets to meet gov thompson on jan 26

3. the recipe called for a tsp of cinnamon and a qt of milk

4. carlos contreras and amelia montoya are in mrs hamiltons class

5. call dr johnson if you cant make your appointment

6. That new boys home is on sixth ave

7. pres clinton is speaking on television fri at 6 30

8. is bob more than 40 in tall now

Write a sentence with each of these abbreviations.

| qt. | Dr. | Mrs. |

_____

_____

_____

Name _____

Who Is Speaking?

Quotation marks show what someone is saying.

"What time is it?" asked Terry.

Circle what is being said.
Underline who is speaking.

1. <u>Mrs. Brown</u> said, "Thank you for helping."

2. "Will you play ball with me?" asked Ted.

3. Maria asked, "Can you come to my party?"

4. "I will have to ask my mother," Tony answered.

5. "The school bus will be here soon," said Arnie.

6. "Don't do that!" shouted the man.

7. "Let's paint a picture for grandma," said Taree.

8. "I don't want liver for dinner," complained Julio.

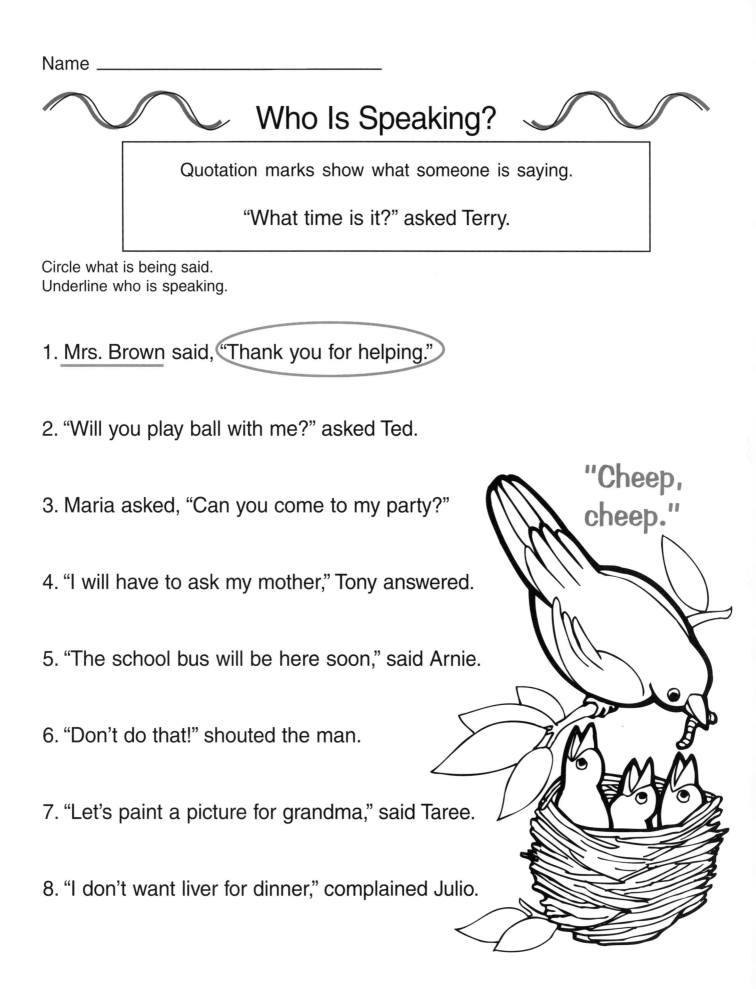

"Cheep, cheep."

Name _____

Quotation Marks

Use quotation marks at the beginning
and at the end of a person's exact words.

"Ssss"

Write each sentence.
Put each person's exact words in quotation marks.

1. Albert said, I'll get us some cookies to eat.

_____

2. Do you have a pet cat? asked William.

_____

3. Mother shouted, Keep away from that spilled paint!

_____

4. Why does Stan get to stay up later than me? complained Harry.

_____

5. Clara said, I want to be a scientist when I grow up.

_____

6. How soon will dinner be ready? asked Father.

_____

A Fishing Trip

Fill in the missing punctuation and capital letters.
Don't forget the quotation marks.

pat and mike were going fishing pat was bringing lunch and mike was bringing the fishing poles and bait

i cant wait to get started this is going to be fun, said mike

wow the fish are almost jumping out of the water, shouted pat mike caught the first fish it was too small to keep mike threw it back into the water

the boys were so busy fishing they forgot the time im getting hungry, announced mike pat was ready for a snack too the boys got out sandwiches cookies and juice

the boys ate fished and played in the stream the rest of the afternoon they started home at 5 00 the last fish I caught was the biggest one, bragged mike it will taste delicious for dinner

         Punctuation EMC 141

Answer Key

Page 1

Circle - 3, 5, 6, 8, 9, 11, 12, 14

8 sentences

Page 2

Circle - 1, 5, 6, 8, 11, 12, 13

7 sentences

Page 3

1. yes
2. no
3. yes
4. yes
5. no
6. yes
7. no
8. yes
9. yes
10. no
11. no
12. yes
13. yes
14. no

8 sentences

Page 4

1. Ted likes to play baseball.
2. the oldest boy.
3. My pet hamster got out of its cage.
4. We all helped wash the car.
5. under the bed.
6. The giraffe ate from the top of the tree.
7. Can you fix the broken toy?
8. margo and her pet dog
9. We ran down the street.
10. Will you order a big pizza?

Page 5

The beaver wanted to build a lodge.
She cut down trees and branches.
a big pile in the pond. ✗
The lodge stuck up above the water.
doorway under the water. ✗
The beaver went into the dry lodge.
This is where the beaver will have her babies.

Page 6

Period after - 1, 4, 5

Page 7

Period after - 1, 2, 3, 6, 7, 9 ,10

Page 8

Question mark after - 1, 2, 3, 4, 6, 7, 9,10

Page 9

Question mark after - 1, 2, 4, 7, 8

Page 10

Question mark after - 1, 3, 4, 6
Student sentences will vary.

Page 11

1. I like to play hopscotch
2. Can you run fast
3. Morris has a pet frog
4. What is in that box
5. Alma has a baby sister
6. Where did the puppy go
7. Will you help me
8. Sandy went swimming

Page 12

1. question mark
2. period
3. question mark
4. period
5. period
6. question mark
7. question mark
8. question mark
9. question mark
10. period
11. period
12. question mark
13. period
14. question mark

Page 13

Dot-to-dot is a dinosaur.

Student sentences will vary.

Page 14

I had a good nap.

Now I am hungry.

I want something to eat.

Is there food under the table?

I think I saw some crumbs there.

The cat is by the door.

Is he asleep?

He looks like he is.

Can I sneak by the cat?

Will he wake up when I go by?

He may be hungry too.

Page 15

Do you like summer?

It is my favorite time of year.

Can you guess why?

I love picnics.

So do all my friends.

Have you ever gone on a picnic?

What food did you take?

Did you drop scraps on the ground?

We find good food when people leave.

Look for me at your next picnic.

Do you think I will be there?

Page 16

1. !
2. !
3. !
4. !
5. !
6. !

Student sentences will vary.

Page 17

! - 1, 4, 5, 6, 9   X - 2, 3, 7, 8, 10

Page 18

1. question mark
2. period
3. exclamation mark
4. question mark
5. period
6. question mark
7. period or exclamation mark
8. question mark

Page 19

Carlos and Mario went on a picnic.

They put their food on the picnic table.

Just as they started to eat a storm started.

The food began to get wet.

Raindrops, raindrops, raindrops **X**

The boys ran for shelter.

Hurrah, the rain stopped!

Could the boys eat lunch now?

Page 20

Student sentences will vary.

Page 21

What is your favorite day of the week?
I like Saturday best.
My friend Tony and I go to the beach.
We climb on the rocks and make sand castles.

Are you a good climber?
I am a good climber.
We like to look in the tide pools.
We find interesting plants and animals.

Have you ever seen a live crab?
Tony found one last week.
Did you know crabs could pinch?
Tony dropped that crab very fast. *or* !
I got too close to the waves last Saturday.

Tony yelled, "Look out!"
It was too late.
Boy, did I get wet! *or* .

Do you want to go with us next time?
Will your mom let you come?
We will let you pick up any crabs we find.
We will have a good time.

Page 22

Look!
It's snowing!
Winter is here at last.
It is cold outside in the snow.
Do you have mittens to keep your fingers warm?
I have red wool mittens.
What kind do you have?
Do you have boots and a hat too?
Can you come to my house to play?
Bring your sled.
We can slide down the hill by the school.
We can make a snow monster later.
Will your mom let you come?
Come on, Mike.
Let's go ask her now.

Page 23

I want some popcorn.
Mom isn't here.
Can we fix it?

Sure, I know how.
I'll get the popper.
You get the popcorn.

Is the popper turned on?

I plugged it in.
Will you put in a cup of popcorn now?
I'll melt some butter.

Wow!
Look at it pop.
It smells so good.
Do you want to eat it outside?

That will be fun.
I'll put the butter on it.
Don't forget the salt.
I can't wait to taste it. *or* !

Page 24

Mom, are you going to town today?
I want to go to the pet shop.
My fish need food.
May I ask Kim to go with us?
She likes to see the animals there.

Do you see all the new kittens?
Aren't they cute?
Which one do you like best?
I like the little one with the black nose.
Oops! He fell on top of the yellow one.

This is all the fish food I need.
Should I get a new bowl too?
I think I'll wait until next time.
Come on, Kim.
We had better hurry.
My mom will be waiting for us.
This has been fun. *or* !
Are you going to come back for a kitten?

Page 25

Why are you laughing?
What is so funny?

Miss Brown brought three frogs to school.
She put them in a glass box.
We named them Ribbit, Hopper, and Max.

That doesn't sound very funny.
What happened?

Pam went to see the frogs.
The lid was off the box.

Max and Hopper got away.
They hopped out the door and down the hall.

That is funny! *or* .
Who left the lid off?

We don't know.
Can you go to the pond with me?
Maybe we can get more frogs.
Ribbit needs friends.

Page 26

What a surprise I had yesterday.
It was a cool day in October.
I was growing in my pumpkin patch.
Two children came over and picked me up.
What was going to happen next?
Why did they want me?

The boy carried me to his wagon.
The children began to pull me down the street.
Where were they taking me?
We came to a house with a wide porch.
The boy cut holes in my side.
Then the girl put a candle inside me.
They sat me in this window.
Why did they leave me here?
It is very dark outside.
Oh, no!
Who are those monsters tapping at the door?

Page 27

Circle - 1, 3, 6, 8, 9, 10, 12

Page 28

1. question mark - question
2. period - statement
3. period - command
4. period - statement
5. exclamation mark - exclamation
6. period - statement
7. question mark - question
8. period - command

Page 29

1. exclamation mark - exclamation
2. question mark - question
3. period - command
4. period - command
5. period - statement
6. exclamation mark - exclamation
7. question mark - question
8. period - statement

Page 30

Sentences will vary.

Page 31

1. My pet is small.
2. It can hop and swim.
3. My pet eats bugs.
4. It is as green as grass.
5. It is a funny pet.
6. Can you tell what my pet is?

The pet is <u>a frog</u>.

Page 32

1. My dog is a poodle. What kind do you have?
2. Is that a cat? No, it is a skunk.
3. Bob can't find his cake. Did Ann eat it?
4. Why did you miss school? Were you sick?
5. Do you like to play hopscotch? I think it's fun.
6. When did you get that toy? Can I play with it?
7. They must go home at 4:30. What time is it now?
8. Grandma is coming today. She will stay a week.
9. How old are you? I am 10.
10. I am going to the movies. Can you come?

Page 33

1. Where did you get that book? Can I read it?
2. I just got to school. Am I late?
3. John has a sandwich for lunch. What do you have?
4. Don't climb up that old ladder. It isn't safe.
5. I like the present you made for me.
6. When are you going to the party? Can I come too?
7. My dentist gave me a new toothbrush.
8. Raul fell off his bike. He broke his arm.
9. Who painted that picture? It is pretty.
10. Please bring me that vase.
    I want to put these flowers in it.

Page 34

1. Can you come over? I need help.
2. My pet mice escaped. Can you help me catch them?
3. Where do you think they went? Did they get outside?
4. Look out! One just ran under your feet.
5. Did it go under that chair? Let's move it and see.
6. I got him. Where is the cage?
7. How many mice do you have? We've found three.
8. That is all. Lock the cage carefully.
9. Would you like to feed them? They like sunflower seeds.
10. Thank you for helping. You're a good friend.

Page 35

1. Can I go out to play?
2. Amy and I gave the dog a bath.
3. I like to eat ice cream.

4. Mom says I have to stay home today.
5. When will I get to have a turn?
6. My sister and I are twins.

Sentences will vary.

Page 36

When I was little I played a color game with my mother.

Every time I saw the color red I would shout "I spy red!" Every day we would look for another color. This is how I learned the names of all the colors.

I still like to look for colors when I take a walk. Only now I look for colors of cars and trucks. It is only a few more years before I can drive a car. I'm already looking for the best color. Maybe I'll get a red one, since it was the first color I ever knew!

Page 37

Help! I can't get away. I am trapped in this net. Will help come soon? How will I escape? It's no fun to be in a net. I want to be back in the water.

What is that? It is a rip in the net. Can I get out that way? The rip isn't big. Will I be able to push my way out? I'm going to try. Here I go!

Page 38

What a strange place this is. It doesn't look like Earth. Why is it so dark? What is that furry shape over there by the rocks? It's moving closer. Help! I can't get away. (or Help, I can't get away!) Why won't my feet move? I'm caught in sticky mud. Can anyone hear me? Hurry! Save me!

What a scary dream! I am glad I woke up. I'm never going to eat a peanut butter and pickle sandwich again!

Page 39

Sally Smith
Jamal Biondi
Raul Martinez
Anna Chin
Salvatore Toscano
Tammy Westwood
Esther Jacobs
Mary Beth Allen

Page 40

1. Margo went to visit her cousins Bill and Ann.
2. Did you see Luis riding on his horse Prince?
3. Columbus sailed across the Atlantic Ocean.
4. Doctor Reyes gave Kathy a shot.
5. Can you help Mrs. Smith mow her lawn?
6. Roy, Tim, and Bill are triplets.

Page 41

Sam has two dogs.
One is a black and white dog named Lady.
The other dog is a frisky puppy named Bubbles.
Bubbles likes to play with Lady.
Sometimes Lady gets tired of Bubbles.
She growls and moves away.
Bubbles will follow Lady and try to play again.
Sam has to take Bubbles to the front yard
so Lady can get some rest.

Page 42

Tommy, your birthday is almost here. You may invite five friends to your party. What do you want to do? Would you like a party at home? I can bake a cake, and you can play games. Choose soon so we can send out the invitations.

Could we go somewhere? Henry took us to the pizza place on his birthday. It was fun! I've got an idea. I would like to take my friends roller-skating. Can we do that? Could we come home after we skate for ice cream and cake? I can't wait! Aren't birthdays wonderful?

Page 43

It is Matt's turn at bat. Will he get a hit?
Matt hit the ball hard. Look at it go!
It is going to the back of the field. Run fast, Matt!
Ted is running after the ball. Can he catch it?
Will Matt make a home run? Oh, no!
Ted got the ball. Matt is not happy to be out.

It is my turn at bat. Will I get a hit?
I want to make a run for my team. I will do my best.

Page 44

1. Sunday
2. Thursday, Friday
3. Saturday
4. Monday
5. Wednesday
6. Tuesday

Answers will vary.

Page 45

January	July
February	August
March	September
April	October
May	November
June	December

Answers will vary.

Page 46

1. We will spend Christmas in Texas with grandmother.
2. Terry gave me a funny card on Valentine's Day.
3. We had a fat turkey for Thanksgiving dinner.
4. Are you going to have fireworks on Independence Day?
5. Mark gave his dad a tie for Father's Day.
6. Mr. Barton's class is learning about Chinese New Year.
7. Do you look for colored eggs on Easter Sunday?
8. We remember George Washington and Abraham Lincoln on Presidents' Day.

Page 47

Marine World
Yosemite National Park
San Francisco
Mississippi River
Bagel Bakery
Museum of Natural History
Jefferson Elementary School
New York
British Columbia
Quick Stop Gas
Broadway Avenue

Page 48

1. In Fairbanks, Alaska, snow stays on the mountains most of the year.
2. I went swimming in Lake Tahoe with my best friend.
3. The library is on Elm Street.
4. Tomorrow we will go to Chicago to see a ball game.
5. Larry was fishing off the wharf in Monterey.
6. Stella traveled to Seattle, Washington, with her family.

Page 49

1. Pedro lives in Santa Monica, California.
2. Carla said, "I am going to Six Flags Over Texas in August."
3. Mrs. Williams was born in Utah, but now she lives in Mexico City.
4. Can I ask Tony and his family over for Easter dinner?

Page 50

1. Columbus, Ohio	4. Memphis, Tennessee
2. Honolulu, Hawaii	5. Santa Barbara, California
3. Toronto, Ontario	6. Whitehorse, Yukon Territory

1. March 31, 1874	4. December 25, 2000
2. July 4, 1776	5. August 22, 1943
3. January 1, 1998	6. November 3, 1800

Page 51

1. March 11, 1998
2. March 6, 1998
3. March 15, 1998
4. March 28, 1998
5. March 4, 1998 and March 18, 1998

Page 52

1. I went to the park with Raul, Mark, and Lou.
2. Grandma planted roses, daisies, and tulips in her garden.
3. The girls ate sandwiches, pickles, and cookies at the picnic.
4. Robins can fly, sing, and build nests.
5. Kangaroos, koalas, and wombats have pouches.
6. Harry, Susan, Will, and Maria sold hotdogs at the football game.
7. Mom fixed peas, corn, and tomatoes for dinner last night.
8. It rained all day on Monday, Tuesday, and Wednesday.

Page 53

1. Clarence will swim, ride, and hike at camp.
2. Mrs. Chin has a wallet, a comb, a mirror, and a lipstick in her purse.
3. Mark has a sandwich, carrot sticks, an apple, and cookies in his lunch.
4. Lonnie got a story book, a bracelet, cowboy boots, and a hamster for her birthday.

Page 54

1. Mosquitos, crickets, and owls kept the campers awake most of the night.
2. We ate turkey, dressing, and gravy at Thanksgiving dinner.
3. I want to plant lettuce, carrots, radishes, and peas in my garden.
4. Lightning flashed, thunder roared, and gusty winds blew during the storm.
5. The children ran through the gate, across the lawn, and into the house.
6. Would you prefer an apple, an orange, or a banana in your lunch?
7. Did you go to Disneyland, Magic Mountain, or Marine World on your vacation?
8. Whales, sharks, tuna, and jellyfish all live in the sea.

Page 55

Answers will vary.

Page 56

Answers will vary.

Page 57

Washington Elementary School
1200 Main Street
Madera, California 93637

Mr. Frank Jones
537 Yosemite Avenue
Eaton, Colorado 80615

Answers will vary.

Page 58

1. Dear Grandma and Grandpa,
2. Dear Juanita,
3. Dear Aunt Mattie,
4. Dear Conrad,
5. Dear Uncle Fred,
6. Dear George,

1. Love,
2. Sincerely,
2. Your friend,
3. Goodbye,

Page 59

Answers will vary.

Page 60

February 18, 1997

Dear Sally,

Thank you for asking me to your Valentine's Day party last Saturday. It was fun playing games with Ann, Margaret, Tonya, and you. It was fun making valentine cards too. Did you have a good time?

I really liked the pink ice cream and punch. Those heart-shaped cookies Mrs. Ramirez made were so pretty. They tasted yummy too. Do you think Ann got to help her mom make them?

My mom says I can have a party on Saint Patrick's Day. Can you come? We will play games and have good things to eat.

Your friend,
Angela

Page 61

Answers will vary.

Punctuation EMC 141

Page 62

1. 6:45
2. 11:25
3. 3:15
4. 9:00
5. 2:30
6. 8:53

1. Arturo has an appointment with Dr. Martin at 4:15.

2. The movie starts at 6:00. Don't be late.

3. Can you get here by 12:00 noon?

4. I went to bed at 9:00 last night. I got up at 7:30 this morning.

5. The plane from New York City will arrive at 2:40.

6. Sam was born at 12:45. His twin brother was born 15 minutes later.

Page 63

1. Dear Mr. President:
2. Dear Cary,
3. Dear Senator Kennedy:
4. Dear Santa Claus,
5. Dear Governor Wilson:
6. Dear Uncle Marcus,

Letters will vary.

Page 64

1. Seattle, Washington
2. April 4, 1776
3. 1:45
4. Calgary, Alberta
5. $1.45
6. February 14, 1990
7. 12:30
8. $11.95
9. Denver, Colorado
10. $240.60
11. November 17, 1996
12. 4:15

I am leaving for Albany, New York. The flight leaves at 6:45 on May 21, 1998. My ticket cost $325.50.

Page 65

1. Sam's lunch
2. Pam's book
3. Ken's ball
4. Pete's bone
5. Lucy's kite
6. Arturo's gift/present

Page 66

1. boys'
2. cooks'
3. farmers'
4. girls'
5. gardeners'
6. workers'

Page 67

can't   won't   let's   he's
it's   they're   you'll   wouldn't
we're   she'll   I'm   there's

1. can't
2. we're
3. I'm
4. won't
5. it's
6. there's
7. let's
8. she'll
9. wouldn't
10. he's
11. they're
12. you'll

Page 68

1. The two girls' sweaters looked the same.

2. That boy's dog can't come in the house.

3. We won't go to my aunt's house until Friday.

4. It's too late to play with Kate's kite.

5. Those workers' tools must be put away.

6. I don't like to eat lima beans.

Red circles:
can't   won't
it's   don't

Green circles:
girls'   boy's
aunt's   kate's
workers'

Page 69

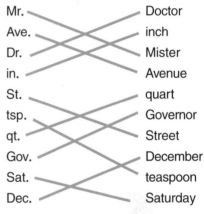

Mr. — Mister
Ave. — Avenue
Dr. — Doctor
in. — inch
St. — Street
tsp. — teaspoon
qt. — quart
Gov. — Governor
Sat. — Saturday
Dec. — December

Page 70

1. Mr. Garcia teaches math at my school.

2. Max gets to meet Gov. Thompson on Jan. 26.

3. The recipe called for a tsp. of cinnamon and a qt. of milk.

4. Carlos Contreras and Amelia Montoya are in Mrs. Hamilton's class.

5. Call Dr. Johnson if you can't make your appointment.

6. That new boy's home is on Sixth Ave.

7. Pres. Clinton is speaking on television Fri. at 6:30.

8. Is Bob more than 40 in. tall now?